STOP
SELLING
START
SERVING

MELVIN WHITE

Acknowledgments

I would like first to thank God for the grace and vision to write this book and to live the experiences that shaped every page.

To my wife, Catrina, who has stood by my side for over thirty years—you are my constant, my encourager, and my greatest blessing. Your strength, faith, and partnership have made every journey worth it.

To my daughter, Dr. Crystal White, whose brilliance, compassion, and drive inspire me daily. Watching you grow into the powerful woman and professional you are has been one of the greatest joys of my life.

To my granddaughter, Isabella—my ball of positive energy and sunshine. Your light keeps me dreaming and believing in the next generation.

And to my mentor and brother, James, who started a dental lab business at just eighteen years old and dedicated his life to building smiles, I dedicate this book in your memory. You were the first person I saw create something out of nothing. You built smiles for others while showing me that life extended far beyond our immediate surroundings. Your example was the blueprint that helped me see what was possible.

James passed away at just forty-nine years old from a major lung illness, but he worked faithfully through it all, staying positive, even while in the hospital. He showed me that real leadership is about serving people consistently, with care and excellence. His life was my first and most personal lesson in servant leadership. He didn't just talk about it; he lived it.

Thank you to every friend, colleague, and leader who encouraged me along the way. This book was written for you—and because of you.

Table of Contents

Introduction

I didn't set out to write a book about selling.

Honestly, I thought I'd write a book about my life. Growing up in Boxtown, Memphis. Sharing how we all squeezed into that little house with one bathroom. Most of the time, we had no hot water unless we boiled it because we couldn't afford a new water heater. Talking about how I started selling candy at five years old and hustled through high school with party tickets and encyclopedias. I even spent a season going down the wrong road in life, doing things I'm not proud of. But I came out of that—by grace—and landed in corporate sales, launching phone stores, and leading teams for Fortune 50 companies.

But as I sat with the idea of writing, I kept coming back to this truth: **the most significant impact I've had in life hasn't come from what I've done, where I've been, or how much I've sold—it's come from how I served.**

This book is more than just pages filled with advice; it's a shift. A shift in how we see sales, how we build trust, and how we create relationships that last. It's about purpose over pitch, people over profit. Because once you stop selling and start serving, everything changes.

So what can you expect in the pages ahead?

We'll start by addressing a harsh truth: the real reasons people don't buy from you. It's not about price, it's about belief, clarity, and connection. We'll unpack how your energy, your clarity, and your intention shape how others receive your message.

We'll dive into the heart of why service should always come before the sale. Whether you're a business owner, a ministry leader, or a side hustler, people respond to those who care, not those who chase. And, we'll define the difference between principles, strategies, and tactics—and why most people get those in the wrong order. Trust me, this one matters more than most think.

We will walk you through what it takes to build absolute trust, how persuasion works when rooted in service, and what servant leadership looks like in your day-to-day work. I hope to show you how to recognize and celebrate small wins, because it's not just the big goals that matter—it's the small, consistent moments of growth that create legacy.

I'll introduce you to the mentors and voices that helped shape my journey—from my big brother James to some of the greats like Les Brown, Eric Thomas, Myron Golden, Lisa Nichols, Jim Rohn, and Tony Dungy. Their examples, and hopefully mine, will remind you that this isn't just a technique—it's a lifestyle. Serving isn't what you do on the clock; it's who you are.

This book will walk you through what I've learned the hard way, the long way, and sometimes the wrong way. But also what I've learned through faith, failure, mentors, and those quiet moments where I had to ask, "Would I buy from me?"

My prayer is that you'll walk away from this with more than better sales results—but with a bigger heart for people and a deeper understanding of what it means to serve truly.

Let's get into it.

CHAPTER 1

The Real Reasons People Don't Buy from You

Before we get into why people say no, let's start by defining what this is really all about.

I'll never forget one of my first lessons in what *not* to do in sales.

Back then, I thought I was ready for anything, new suit, clean cut, full of confidence. I'd memorized every detail about the product: the features, the price points, ten reasons why anyone should say yes. I figured I was going to knock it out of the park.

I walked into a boutique in Memphis and launched into my pitch. I unloaded every detail I knew, rattling off benefits no one had asked about, answering questions no one had raised. It sounded less like a conversation and more like an audition.

After a moment, the owner stopped me and asked, "Have you ever thought about asking what I actually need?"

That question hit me like a brick. I realized I wasn't listening; I was checking boxes. I was trying to talk someone into a decision I wanted them to make instead of helping them make a choice they were already considering for their own reasons.

That was the day I stopped thinking about "selling" and started focusing on serving.

What is Sales?

Sales helps people make a decision they already want to make—for their own reasons. It's not about talking someone into something they don't want. It's not convincing. It's not coercion. Great salespeople don't pressure—they guide. They listen, ask the right questions, and help people move confidently toward what they already want.

What is Serving?

Serving is putting the other person's interests first, even if it doesn't benefit you right away. It means showing up with empathy, listening without agenda, and offering value before asking for anything in return.

Serving is rooted in trust. It's not about the transaction—it's about the transformation.

When you combine sales and serving, you stop chasing commissions and start creating connections.
You stop trying to close people and start helping them open doors they already want to walk through.

So why, then, do people say no when they might otherwise say yes?

Reason Number One: They don't believe you.

And the reason they don't believe you is because of the way you're presenting your message. Your delivery is telling them not to believe you. Not to trust you. Not to see you as an answer to anything but as an interruption to their day.

What does that even mean? Well, when people look at you, it's not through their own eyes but yours.

Proverbs says,

> *"As in water, face answereth to face, so doth the heart of man to man." That means, just like when you look in water and see your reflection, people see a reflection of how you see yourself. You reflect on others how you see yourself.*

So if you want people to believe you, you've got to start by believing yourself—believing in what you're selling, the result it can produce, and the value it delivers. Because here's the truth: you can lie with your words, but your energy always tells the truth.

And maybe the reason you don't believe in what you're doing is that you don't trust yourself. Perhaps you've broken too many promises to yourself in the past. And that shows up in how you sell. Or maybe you don't trust your product or service. You know it doesn't work. You know for every ten sales, there are nine complaint calls. Or perhaps you've never used the product or service, so you don't have experiential belief in it.

People go through life making choices. Not decisions. A choice means you pick something for now. A decision, from the Latin root "de" meaning "off" and "cision" meaning "to cut," means you cut off every other option. When you decide, it's real. There is no turning back. You are like warriors who sailed to an island to fight their enemy; when they landed ashore, they burned their ships. That's a decision. Most people haven't decided.

Reason Number Two: They don't understand.

The biggest mistake in communication is thinking it happened at all. Just because you said words doesn't mean your prospect heard them the way you intended. People don't hear your words; they hear their interpretation of your words filtered through their past experiences, their current mood, and a dozen other things.

That's why you've got to be clear. Define your terms. Avoid buzzwords, tech lingo, and vague language. Words like "solutions" or "development" sound good but mean different things to different people.

If I say "trauma," you might think of a bad conversation with your mom. Someone else thinks of an active war zone. Same word, different dictionaries. A sales campaign may offer an entry into a drawing for a trip to New York City. To one person, that may conjure up images of limousines, bright lights, and Broadway shows. To someone who was mugged in New York eight years ago, it will conjure up a completely different image.

You've got to know what your prospect wants. And then, you've got to communicate that you have it. Speak in plain language. Even better, paint word pictures. Don't just "sell shoes." Say, "I've got a pair of shoes that'll make you feel like you stepped out of GQ." That image sticks.

Reason Number Three: They smell commission breath.

What's that? It's the stench of desperation. When you're so thirsty to close a deal, people can feel it. And human nature is funny; we run from desperation but chase what seems just out of reach.

If you are in financial straits or have some heavy-handed manager pressing you to meet a quote, it will come through your communication, appearance, eye contact, and demeanor.

So don't lean in so hard that people lean away. Remember: **you have the goods**. You're the one with the value. Whether they say yes or no, you're okay. I like to say, "If they say yes, congratulations. If they say no, congratulations. Either way, I'm so cool with it, I don't wanna fool with it."

Stop chasing people. Start becoming more visible to the people who already want what you have. Think of yourself as a waiter in a crowded restaurant holding the pitcher of lemonade. You don't force it on the diners. You simply go from table to table, looking for the thirsty ones, and ask, "Would you like a refill?" It doesn't matter to you if they say yes or no. Thirsty people always say yes, and people who don't drink lemonade will always say no.

Let me be even more direct: if people don't *want* what you offer, no pitch—no matter how smooth—is going to move them. You can't force your way into someone's wallet. But you *can* earn their trust.

Reason Number Four: They don't see the need.

A common mistake in sales is assuming that "everybody needs this." That's false. Outside of food, water, and air, very few things are universal needs. So quit thinking your offer is for everyone. You may have the best widget on the planet. But you're setting yourself (and your prospects) up for an awkward conversation if you hype it like it's something everyone should want.

Let me give you a real example from the world of cell phones.

When I first got into the wireless industry, I believed with all my heart that **everyone** needed a phone. I pushed the product hard. But, over time, I learned an important distinction: it's not the device everyone needs. I had the message a bit distorted. What people really needed were the things the device allowed them to do.

Cell phones became valuable not just for making calls. They already had phones that could do that. The real value lay in how they helped people stay connected. Connected to everything: to business opportunities, to real-time information, and most importantly, to the people they loved. Staying in touch with family, calling for help, checking on children, sending money to a loved one—*that was* the value. The phone was just the tool.

According to Statista, over 4.2 billion people as of 2024 now use smartphones. But even with that number, it doesn't mean it's a universal "need." However, it does mean that the perceived value is strong enough for that number of people to say "yes."

So, your job isn't to convince people they <u>need</u> your product. Your job is to help them connect your offer to a real outcome in their lives. A want becomes a need when the value is clear.

Reason Number Five: They don't believe it's worth the money.

Sometimes the issue isn't the price they'll have to pay if they say yes; it's that you haven't helped them consider the cost of staying stuck. The cost of missing out. The cost of doing nothing.

People get so focused on "how much is this going to cost me?" that they never ask, "What will it cost me if I don't move forward?"

When someone asks me how much something costs, I stop answering and, instead, ask, "Are you asking how much it costs if you say yes or how much it costs if you say no?" That question changes everything.

Because if your solution helps them avoid wasting time, losing money, or missing opportunities, not buying might actually be the most expensive decision of all.

Now let's talk about value. Every offer you present has two types of value: intrinsic value (what it actually does) and perceived value (how it makes someone feel).

People will often pay more for how something makes them feel than for what it does. A car is a car. But why does one person pay $30,000 for a vehicle and another pay $300,000? The tires don't roll faster. The air conditioner isn't ten times colder. The difference? Perceived value.

The same is true with luxury brands. Take Louis Vuitton belts, for example. Many of them are crafted from coated canvas—a material composed of polyvinyl chloride (PVC) and polyurethane (PU)—rather than full-grain leather. Despite this, they command prices upwards of $795. Why? Because the LV initials carry status, Louis Vuitton has mastered the art of selling identity, not just a product.

If you want to raise your close rate, don't rush to discount. Instead, **increase the perceived value**. Paint the picture. Connect the dots. Help them feel what they gain—and what they lose—based on their decision.

Here's another way to look at it: Let's say you're offering a tool or service that saves someone five hours a week. If their time is worth $50 an hour, that's $250 a week—or $13,000 a year. But your product costs $1,200. On the surface, they see the $1,200 price tag. But when you walk them through the cost of not saying yes, suddenly they realize they're losing $13,000 to save $1,200. That's when the light bulb goes off.

Or here's a real-life example from my own experience. I once had a business owner hesitate on investing in credit card processing for his restaurant. He only saw the 2–5% transaction fee as a loss. But what he wasn't calculating was the cost of lost customers— people who didn't carry cash and would walk out. I asked him, "How much are you losing every weekend just because someone couldn't pay the way they wanted to?" When he did the math, the fee became a small cost in exchange for much bigger gains.

You don't just sell the value of saying yes; you help them feel the cost of saying no.

Reason Number Six: They didn't participate in the presentation.

If you're doing all the talking, they're doing all the doubting.

Too many salespeople treat their pitch like a performance. They rehearse, present, and "deliver" like they're on stage. But let me tell you something: **sales should never be a monologue**. It's a conversation—a dance. And like any good dance, both people must be in step.

You've got to get them involved. Ask questions. Listen deeply. Respond with curiosity. When someone gives you an answer, dig a little deeper. Ask, *"Tell me more about that."*
Not only does it show that you care—it gives them a chance to process their own needs out loud.

Here's the truth: **The more they say, the more likely they are to buy. The more they do, the more emotionally invested they become.**

Whether you're in a one-on-one meeting, a Zoom call, or a room full of people, make space for their voice. Use prompts like:

- *"Type YES in the chat if this resonates with you."*

- *"Raise your hand if this challenge sounds familiar."*

- *"On a scale from 1 to 10, how important is solving this right now?"*

Participation turns presentation into engagement—and engagement builds trust. And trust? That's what leads to decisions.

You want them to talk *with* you, not just listen *to* you.

Fix any one of these reasons, and your sales will improve. Fix all of them? **You'll be unstoppable.**

"You can have everything in life you want, if you will just help enough other people get what they want."

— Zig Ziglar

CHAPTER 2

The Heart of Business—Serving, Not Selling

Too many businesses focus on closing deals, hitting quotas, and making sales. But the real secret to long-term success? **Serving.** When you shift from a selling mindset to a serving mindset, everything changes—your relationships, your reputation, and most importantly, your results.

People don't want to be sold to. They want to feel heard, valued, and understood. They want solutions, not sales pitches. The businesses that thrive understand this fundamental truth: **when you put service first, sales follow naturally.**

> *"Whoever wants to become great among you must be your servant, and whoever wants to be first must be your slave—just as the Son of Man did not come to be served, but to serve, and to give his life as a ransom*

for many."
—Matthew 20:26-28 (NIV)

The Shift: From Transactional to Transformational

Too many entrepreneurs and sales professionals operate with a transactional mindset—focused on the numbers, the commission, and the immediate win. But true business success comes from **transformational relationships**. This means:

- **Understanding the real needs** of your clients, not just what you want to sell to them.

- **Providing solutions** that genuinely help them, even if it doesn't immediately result in a sale.

- **Building trust** by putting their best interests first.

When you serve people, you don't just make a sale—you make an impact. And in return, your business grows in ways you never imagined.

> *"Service is the rent we pay for the privilege*
> *of living on this earth."*
> *—Shirley Chisholm*

In order to do this effectively, you must be thinking about the long game, not the quick win. If this product isn't best for your prospect right now, perhaps something you offer down the line will be. If you serve them rather than your own interests, you can all but guarantee a sale later.

"I would love to sell these solar panels. But I heard you say that your mom is sick and that you are planning to spend half the year in Boston taking care of her, while your sister covers the other half. It would take you much longer to break even on these panels, and this is the smallest system we currently offer. I'm sorry, but it wouldn't be a good deal for you to switch from electric power right now."

Now imagine returning a year later with a smaller system that is perfect for the client. You already know their story. You've already built rapport. And they trust you completely. You can sell them the smaller system now, and an upgrade when they return to living full-time in their home state. That's selling to serve.

Serve First, Sell Later

If you want to win in business, you must prioritize service over sales. Selling is about convincing, but **serving is about connecting**. When you lead with service:

- People come to you because they trust you.

- You create long-term clients instead of one-time buyers.

- You build a reputation that attracts more opportunities.

Real-World Example: TOMS Shoes—Serving Through Business

One of the best examples of how service drives success is **TOMS Shoes**. When Blake Mycoskie founded the company in 2006, he didn't just start another shoe brand; he built a **mission-driven business.**

TOMS created a **"One for One" model**: for every pair of shoes a customer bought, the company **gave another pair to a child in need.** This wasn't just a marketing gimmick. It was a movement.

- **People didn't just buy TOMS because they liked the shoes.** Of course, they loved the shoes. But they loved lots of companies' shoes. They could have purchased shoes anywhere. But they bought from Toms for more than shoes. They bought into the vision, the purpose, the impact.

- **Customers became loyal advocates,** sharing the brand's mission with others.

- **The company scaled rapidly,** selling millions of shoes while giving away millions more.

TOMS proved that serving isn't just the right thing to do—it's a **winning business strategy.** When customers see that a company genuinely cares about making a difference, they're more likely to support it.

This same principle applies to any business. Whether you're selling products or services, your success depends on **how well you serve others.** When people feel valued, they don't just buy from you once—they **stick with you** and bring others along with them.

Because here's the truth: **You don't chase success. You attract it.** And the way you attract it? **By leading with service.**

So, how are you going to start serving today?

The Many Forms of Serving in Business

Serving isn't just about giving away free products or discounts. **True service** is about **adding value** in ways that build relationships, establish trust, and create long-term success. It comes in different forms, many of which we will cover. But, perhaps, the most important is teaching. Decided to be a guide to your prospects today. Teaching comes before selling. That's how you create trust.

How Deep Interest in a Customer's Business Builds Trust

People **buy from those they trust**, and trust is built through **genuine interest**. When you take the time to understand a customer's needs, struggles, and goals, it shows you're not just there for a quick sale. Asking meaningful questions like:

- "What's the biggest challenge in your business right now?"

- "Where do you see your company in the next five years?"

- "What would make your job easier?"

These questions show you're **paying attention to** and **care about their success,** not just your own. The more interest you show, the stronger the relationship becomes—and strong relationships lead to repeat business, referrals, and **loyalty that no discount can match.**

Putting the Customer's Best Interests First Pays Off

When a salesperson puts **profits over people,** customers can feel it. They sense when they're just a number in a system. But when you genuinely prioritize their best interests, **they remember.** Here's what happens when you lead with service instead of sales:

- **Customers feel valued, not pressured.**

- **They trust your recommendations and return for more.**

- **They refer you to others because they know you have integrity.**

The best salespeople don't **push products**—they **solve problems**. When you approach business with a service mindset, your **reputation grows,** and so does your success.

Examples of Serving Across Industries

- **Real Estate: Educating Before Selling**

A good real estate agent doesn't just show homes—they educate buyers on market trends, financing options, and what to look for in a property. They might offer a free seminar on "Buying Your First Home" without expecting attendees to buy immediately. The result? People remember their friendliness and appreciate the information they provided. People trust them when they're ready to purchase.

- **Technology Services: Providing Solutions, Not Just Products**

A great IT consultant doesn't just sell software; they help businesses streamline operations, secure data, and improve efficiency. Offering free security assessments or best-practice guides builds trust and proves expertise. Later, when the customer is ready to buy, they choose someone who already helped them.

- ## Church Services: Serve First, Then Ask

Imagine walking into a church and, before the choir sings, before the sermon, before a single prayer, you're asked for an offering. How would that feel? It would feel transactional, not spiritual.

That's why most churches start with service first. The choir sings, the congregation gives praise, and the pastor delivers a word that feeds the soul. Only then does the offering come. And when it does, people give not out of obligation, but out of gratitude.

But when churches flip it, people would feel like money matters more than the message. That's how it feels in business when someone tries to "close" before they've served. Service builds connection. Connection builds trust. Trust leads to support.

- ## Insurance: Protecting Before Selling

A good insurance agent doesn't just push policies; they educate people on risk management, long-term financial security, and how to protect their families. They might offer a free consultation on "How to Prepare for Retirement" or "What You Need to Know About Life Insurance" without pressuring anyone to buy. That way, when someone is ready, they choose the person who already helped them.

Final Thought: Serve First, and Everything Else Follows

No matter the industry, the principle is the same: **serve first, sell later.** When you make **service the foundation**, success isn't just possible—it's inevitable.

For even the Son of Man did not come to be served, but to serve, and to give his life as a ransom for many. "
— Matthew 20:28 (NIV)

This verse reminds us that the foundation of authentic leadership and success lies in service. When we lead by serving others, everything else follows naturally.

CHAPTER 3

Implementing Servant Leadership in Your Sales Team

"Whoever wants to become great among you must be your servant." — Matthew 20:26

In today's fast-paced, results-driven world, the idea of *serving* others in leadership can feel countercultural. But that's precisely the point. **Servant leadership flips the script**—it says success isn't measured by how many people report to you, but by how well you take care of the people you lead.

This concept has been around for thousands of years. In fact, Jesus modeled it perfectly. And one of the most powerful books that breaks this down in a practical way is *Jesus, CEO* by Laurie Beth Jones. In it, she highlights how Jesus led not with ego, but with empathy, not with a crown, but with a towel. He washed feet, broke bread, and met people where they were. That's not just leadership—that's servant leadership.

What Is Servant Leadership?

Biblically Speaking...

Servant leadership is rooted in scripture. Jesus didn't come to earth to be served, but to serve—and He made that clear:

> *"For even the Son of Man did not come to be served, but to serve, and to give his life as a ransom for many." — Mark 10:45*

He was fully capable of calling down legions of angels, yet He chose humility. He chose compassion. He chose people. That's servant leadership at its core.

Practically Speaking...

Servant leadership means you lead with your team in mind—not from above them, but alongside them. It's not about doing their work or rescuing them from every tough spot. It's about:

- **Empowering** them to grow.

- **Creating a space** where they can thrive.

- **Coaching** instead of commanding.

- **Listening** deeply before speaking.

It means you're willing to have the hard conversations, give the encouragement they need, and sometimes be a quiet presence when they feel overwhelmed.

Modern-Day Examples of Everyday Servant Leaders

We often think of leadership as being reserved for people with titles—pastors, CEOs, managers. And yes, pastors lead, but they also serve as shepherds and teachers, not just from the pulpit, but in prayer, in hospital visits, in sitting with people through grief and struggle.

And what about the waiter at your favorite restaurant? The nurse on the night shift? The single mom who leads her home with strength and compassion? These are servant leaders, too.

The truth is, you don't need a title to be a servant leader. You just need a heart to serve.

How to Serve Your Team (Without Doing Their Job for Them)

One of the biggest misconceptions about servant leadership is that it means being soft or doing everything for your team. That's not it. Serving your team doesn't mean solving every problem—it means equipping them to solve it themselves and walking alongside them every step of the way. Here's how you do that:

✅ Create a Culture of Ownership

Empower your team to take initiative. Ask questions like:

- "What do you think is the best way to handle this?"

- "How can I support you in moving this forward?"

✅ Be Present Without Hovering

Show up. Not just when numbers are down, or problems pop up. Celebrate wins. Check in intentionally. Don't just ask, "How are you doing on your numbers?" Ask, "How are *you* doing?"

✅ Coach, Don't Rescue

If someone's struggling, resist the urge to jump in and fix it. Instead, guide them:

- Help them think through solutions.

- Encourage them to reflect on what worked and what didn't.

- Remind them of their strengths and past successes.

✓ Model What You Want to Multiply

People don't follow what you say. They follow what you *do*. If you want your team to serve your customers well, you need to serve your team well. That means staying consistent, showing integrity, and treating everyone with dignity—especially when no one's watching. Example: The Coffee Spill in Scranton

It was a cold January morning in Lancaster, Pennsylvania.

Snow flurries were dancing across the parking lot as I walked into one of our retail sales offices before the team arrived.

Inside, the lights were dim, the floor mats were wet, and the smell of fresh coffee filled the air.

The manager was already there, straightening displays and vacuuming the lobby.

He wasn't in a meeting or giving a speech. He was quietly preparing the space for his people.

As he turned toward the front door, he spotted a half-spilled cup of coffee that had leaked across the tile near the entrance.

Without missing a beat, he set down his clipboard, grabbed paper towels, and got on his knees to clean it up.

29

No frustration. No orders barked—just action.

A few minutes later, another early employee walked in. She saw the manager crouched on the floor and immediately said,

"Hey, let me help you with that."

He smiled and said,

"You're good. I want the place to look right when everyone walks in."

By 9:00 a.m., the whole team had arrived.

Before the first customer even stepped through the door, one rep started reorganizing the brochure rack.

Another noticed fingerprints on the glass door and wiped them off.

Someone else straightened the chairs in the waiting area.

No one was told to.

They were following what they saw.

By the end of the day, that Lancaster team had posted one of their strongest sales weeks of the quarter.

But the real win wasn't in the numbers—it was in the example.

Excellence had been modeled, not mandated.

Culture had been caught, not taught.

Reflection

That morning taught me something about leadership I've never forgotten:

People don't follow what you say—they follow what you show.

Leadership is contagious, for better or worse.

If you want your team to serve your customers with excellence, serve your team the same way.

That means showing consistency when no one's looking, staying humble enough to handle the small things, and modeling integrity in the moments that don't make the metrics.

Because when leaders kneel to serve, teams rise to lead.

Biblical Principle

> *"Whoever wants to become great among you must be your servant." — Matthew 20:26 (NIV)*

Authentic leadership doesn't start on a stage—it begins on the floor.

It's found in the hands that clean the spill, the heart that sees what others ignore, and the humility that says, "If it matters to them, it matters to me."

That's how servant leaders shape not just results, but people—and that's how people, in turn, build lasting results.

Real Leadership Is About Real People

When I led sales teams, I found this to be true repeatedly: People don't want to be managed. They want to be led. And more than anything, they want to be seen, heard, and valued.

I used to tell my team, "I'm not here to do your job for you, but I will never leave you alone in the work."

That's servant leadership.

It's not soft. It's strong. It's not passive. It's intentional.

And in sales—where pressure can be high, and results can swing—having a leader who serves, not controls, makes all the difference.

Lead Like Jesus, Live as You Care

Leadership is a privilege, not a platform. And when you start with the heart of a servant, everything changes. Your team grows. Your culture thrives. And your impact multiplies.

> *"Leadership is not about being in charge. It's about taking care of those in your charge." — Simon Sinek.*

So if you're leading a team right now, ask yourself: Am I here to be served... or am I here to serve?

Because the answer to that question will define not just your leadership—but your legacy.

Tying It All Together: Stop Selling, Start Serving—Even as a Leader

Let's go back to the heart of this book: **Stop Selling, Start Serving.**

At the beginning, I shared how this idea changed the way I approached not just sales, but life. It's not just a catchy title, it's a **way of thinking, leading, and living.**

And here's the key: **Servant leadership is where that mindset becomes a movement.**

When you're in leadership, it's easy to fall back into the "selling" mentality, selling your expectations, selling the company's goals, selling the numbers. But your team doesn't need to be sold. They need to be served just as your customers do.

They don't need more pressure. They need more purpose.

They don't need more demand. They need more **development**.

They don't need a boss. They need a leader who sees them, supports them, and helps them grow into everything they were created to be.

From Selling Results to Serving People

When I first stepped into leadership at Comcast Business, I quickly realized I couldn't lead everyone the same way. I had to lead collectively but know them individually.

Some of my reps crushed it on the phones. Others came alive in face-to-face meetings. Some were natural at networking events. And others just had a personal, relational gift that made people trust them right away.

So I stopped trying to "sell" them my way of doing it—and I started serving each person according to their strengths.

The results?

- Morale went up.

- Performance improved.

- Loyalty deepened.

- And the culture became something people wanted to be a part of—not just work for.

True Success Comes When You Stop Selling and Start Serving

Whether you're in a sales role, a leadership position, or both, you've got to understand this:

> *You don't build great teams by pushing people. You make them by serving people.*

The companies and leaders who make the most significant impact aren't the ones who shout the loudest or sell the hardest. They're the ones who create environments where people can thrive—because they're seen, supported, and served.

Just like I said from the beginning:

> *When you stop selling and start serving, success doesn't just happen for you; it happens through you.*

It's not a tactic.
It's not a short-term play.
It's a **principle**. A **natural law**. A **biblical truth**.

> *"If serving is beneath you, then leadership is beyond you."*
> *— Unknown*

So, as a leader, the question isn't:
How can I get more out of my team?

The real question is:
How can I pour more into them?

Because when your team knows you're there to serve—not to control, not to impress, not to chase numbers—they'll give you more than effort.

They'll give you **trust**.

And with trust, you'll build something that lasts far beyond any sales goal.

CHAPTER 4

Principles, Strategies, and Tactics

When I first entered the corporate world, I was thrown into a fast-paced environment that lived and breathed strategies and tactics. Everything was about hitting numbers, driving results, launching the next campaign, or fine-tuning the next pitch. And don't get me wrong—those things matter. But I noticed something early on: no matter how solid the tactic or how clever the strategy, they never stuck unless they were grounded in something more profound. That "something" was principles.

Too often, companies hang their values on the wall in a framed vision statement but abandon those same values when the pressure hits. That's when I realized: it's not the strategy that makes the team great; it's the principles they live by. Strategies can change. Tactics can evolve. But principles? They're the foundation. And when you get your principles right, everything else falls into place naturally.

One of the first books that shaped this mindset for me was *The Greatest Salesman in the World* by Og Mandino. In it, he discusses affirming principles such as "I will persist until I succeed." That line hit me hard because no strategy in the world can carry you if your mindset—the principle, strategies, and tactics behind your action—isn't solid.

Let's break down these three key elements:

- **Principles**

Principles are the fundamental truths and values that guide your actions and decisions. They represent the "why" behind everything you do.

Example: A company might commit to principles such as honesty, integrity, and perseverance. For instance, the principle "I will persist until I succeed" from Mandino's classic illustrates how a deep commitment to persistence can be the cornerstone of success in any endeavor.

- **Strategies**

Strategies are the overarching plans or approaches designed to achieve long-term goals. They provide direction and are built on the foundation of your principles.

Example: A business strategy could be to expand into a new market by focusing on customer trust and service excellence. This strategy is rooted in the principle of putting the customer's needs first and aligns with the idea that success comes from genuine engagement rather than short-term wins.

- **Tactics**

Tactics are the specific day-to-day actions or steps taken to execute your strategy. They are the practical measures that move you closer to your goal.

Example: In a sales organization, tactics might include following up with potential clients through personalized emails, hosting informative webinars, or running targeted promotional campaigns. Each tactic supports the broader strategy of building long-term relationships based on trust.

Natural Laws, Sowing & Reaping, and the Foundation of Serving

Above all, natural laws are the proper foundation of everything we do. Consider the law of gravity: if you jump off a tall building, you're going to hit the ground. There's no escaping that truth. Similarly, the law of sowing and reaping is undeniable. You can't expect a harvest if you don't plant a seed. I learned this firsthand from my grandfather and father, who were farmers. Their success depended on understanding and respecting these natural laws.

This principle applies directly to sales, especially when we talk about serving instead of selling. **Serving is like planting seeds.** When you provide genuine value—sharing knowledge, offering help, and putting your customer's best interests first—you're sowing seeds of trust and goodwill. Over time, as these seeds grow, you reap the benefits in the form of loyal customers and sustainable success.

Summary of Principles, Strategies, and Tactics:

- **Principles** are the fundamental truths that guide us, much like natural laws.

- **Strategies** are the plans we develop based on these truths.

- **Tactics** are the specific actions we take to implement our strategies.

When your business is built on strong, unwavering principles—much like the natural law of sowing and reaping—your strategies and tactics will be more effective and authentic. Instead of focusing solely on selling, you begin with serving, ensuring that every interaction plants a seed that can grow into a lasting relationship.

In essence, just as you cannot defy gravity or expect a harvest without sowing, you cannot achieve true business success without serving first. By understanding and aligning with these natural laws, you set the stage for a cycle of service that naturally leads to sales—and sustainable, long-term success.

CHAPTER 5

Know, Like, and Trust: The Foundation of Customer Loyalty

At the heart of customer loyalty lies a simple yet powerful concept: **know, like, and trust**. This idea is based on three essential steps in building meaningful relationships:

- **Know:** Customers first need to know who you are, your background, your values, and what you offer. It's about clear communication and consistent presence.

- **Like:** Once they know you, they need to like you. This comes from authentic interactions where you show empathy, share common ground, and demonstrate that you genuinely care about their needs.

- **Trust:** When customers both know and like you, trust naturally follows. Trust is built when you consistently act

41

in their best interests and deliver on your promises.

A Personal Example: My Experience with Cynthia

Let me share a personal story. For nearly 35 years, I've been getting my hair cut by Cynthia. I didn't know her when I first started. She was introduced to me through a friend's recommendation. Over the decades, I've come to know Cynthia not just as a hairstylist but as someone who consistently makes me feel valued and understood. I trust her implicitly because I know she always strives to make me "look better." This relationship embodies the "know, like, and trust" factor perfectly. Cynthia's genuine care and commitment to serving my needs have made me a loyal customer, illustrating that prioritizing service creates a bond that lasts a lifetime.

> *"I've learned that people will forget what you said, people will forget what you did, but people will never forget how you made them feel."*
> *— Maya Angelou*

By focusing on serving others, putting their needs first, and building relationships through authentic interactions, we lay the groundwork for sustainable success. When customers know, like, and trust you, loyalty follows naturally, and so does long-term prosperity.

Breaking Down Know, Like, and Trust

- **Know:**
  To honestly know someone means understanding their story, values, and challenges. You learn and remember their names. This means engaging with customers in ways that go beyond transactional interactions. It involves listening carefully and learning about their needs.
  Example: When I first met Cynthia, I didn't just see her as someone who could cut my hair; I learned about her passion for her craft and her commitment to making each client feel their best.

- **Like:**
  Liking someone comes naturally when you share authentic experiences. It's about finding common ground and building a rapport that makes both parties feel comfortable and valued.
  Over the decades, I've come to appreciate(like) Cynthia not merely for her skills but also for her genuine care and warm personality. I look forward to each visit because I know she values me as a person.

- **Trust:**
  Trust is the culmination of being known and liked. It is earned when actions consistently reflect integrity and commitment to the other's well-being. Trust transforms one-time interactions into lasting relationships.
  Example: After 35 years of reliable service and genuine care, I trust Cynthia completely with my appearance,

knowing that she always has my best interests at heart.

Prioritizing Customer Needs Over Personal Gains

In every interaction, putting the customer's best interests ahead of personal gain is essential. When customers see that you genuinely care about their needs, they not only return but also become advocates for your service.

The Power of Serving: Know, Like, and Trust in Action

When you serve with authenticity, you create an environment where customers feel valued, understood, and cared for. This approach naturally leads to the know, like, and trust factor, which forms the bedrock of loyalty.

Consider embracing biblical principles of love, faithfulness, and service by prioritizing the genuine needs of those you serve. You will build lasting relationships that withstand the test of time. Whether it's in real estate, technology services, insurance, or even in the humble setting of a local barbershop, when people know you, like you, and trust you, true loyalty is formed.

Remember: the foundation of every lasting relationship is service, not selling. When you serve first, every other success follows naturally.

Effective Communication with Customers

How we communicate is key to building lasting relationships. However, specific commonly used terms can sometimes hinder genuine engagement.

Why Avoid Certain Terms?

Phrases like **"follow-up," "checking in,"** or **"touching base"** might sound professional, but they often come off as impersonal or transactional. When we use these phrases, we risk reducing our interactions to mere routine tasks rather than meaningful connections. They imply that our goal is to tick a box rather than to understand and support our customers truly.

Alternative Approaches for Re-engaging Customers

Instead of relying on generic terms, consider these approaches:

- **Personalize Your Communication:**
  Reference previous conversations or specific details that show you remember and value the customer's unique situation.
  Example: "I was reflecting on our last discussion about your upcoming project, and I have some new ideas that might really work for you."

- **Express Genuine Interest:**
  Show that you care about the customer's well-being and success.

Example: "I've been thinking about how things have been going for you and would love to hear about any new challenges or wins you've experienced."

- **Provide Value:**
   Share insights, updates, or helpful resources that are relevant to the customer's needs.
   Example: "I came across an article that I believe could offer some fresh perspective on your current challenges—would you like me to send it over?"

Personal Example: The "Know, Like, and Trust" Factor

When I think about how absolute trust develops in business, I often think of Shahid.

Back when I worked in the bank card processing business, Shahid owned several gas stations across the city.
At first, our relationship was purely professional.
He didn't really know me, and I was just another vendor trying to earn his business.
But something changed the day I stopped focusing on what I wanted to sell—and started focusing on what he needed to grow.

I noticed his stations had loyal local traffic, but they weren't attracting as many new customers as they could.
Instead of leading with a pitch, I asked questions.
"How are most people paying?"
"What hours are busiest?"
"What challenges are you seeing at the counter?"

He shared openly, and I offered a few small, practical suggestions —none of which benefited me directly. I recommend better signage near the pumps, a rewards program for frequent customers, and a few ways to speed up checkout. He implemented those changes, and within a few months, business picked up noticeably.

From there, our conversations became more frequent—and more personal. We started talking not just about transactions, but about family, faith, and the future. What began as a sales call turned into shared meals, coffee, and laughs, and eventually into a friendship that crossed cultures and backgrounds.

He invited me to his home, and I welcomed him to mine. We got to know each other's families. He didn't just become a client—he became a friend.

And it all started with a straightforward decision: to serve first, without expectation.

Reflection

Trust doesn't happen when you close a sale—it happens when you open a relationship. People don't follow your product; they follow your posture. When you lead with genuine care, people see it. And when they realize your interest goes beyond your invoice, you move from vendor to valued partner.

That's what happened with Shahid.

He didn't need another salesperson—he needed someone who saw his business through his eyes. That's how "know, like, and trust" takes root: not through persuasion, but through partnership.

Biblical Principle

"Do nothing out of selfish ambition or vain conceit. Rather, in humility value others above yourselves." — Philippians 2:3 (NIV)

When you lead with humility, you build bridges that money can't buy. Serving others with sincerity plants seeds that outlast contracts, commissions, and competition. Because in the end, the greatest return on service isn't profit—it's people.

As we move forward, remember that effective communication is not about following a script or using the right buzzwords. It's about connecting on a human level—building relationships that are rooted in authenticity and genuine care.

"If you want to lift yourself, lift someone else."
— Booker T. Washington

This quote perfectly encapsulates our approach: focus on serving others first, and everything else will naturally follow.

Reminding Potential Customers of Organizational Impact

One of the most powerful tools in your communication toolkit is the ability to remind potential customers of the lasting impact your product or service can have on their company. In today's busy business environment, decision-makers are often juggling multiple priorities. Reiterate how your offering aligns with their strategic goals to help ensure that the value remains front and center in their minds.

Why is this the heart of serving

- **Clarity of Benefits:**
  Re-emphasizing impact helps potential customers see beyond your product or service's features, focusing instead on the tangible benefits—such as increased efficiency, cost savings, or improved employee morale—that directly contribute to their organization's success.

- **Building a Compelling Narrative:**
  Every follow-up communication should tell a story that connects your solution to their business challenges. When potential customers understand how your offering can solve their problems or elevate their performance, they're more likely to invest in the relationship.

- **Staying Top of Mind:**
  Regular, value-driven communication helps your brand stand out in a crowded market. When you consistently remind potential customers of the impact your solution

can have, you build trust and reinforce the long-term benefits of choosing to work with you.

Examples of Re-Emphasizing Value in Follow-Up Communications

1. **Success Stories and Case Studies:**
   "I wanted to share how one of our clients in your industry increased their operational efficiency by 30% after implementing our solution. Imagine the potential impact on your organization's bottom line."

2. **Data-Driven Insights:**
   "Based on recent market trends, organizations that adopt our technology have seen a 25% reduction in downtime. This could translate into significant cost savings for you over the next fiscal year."

3. **Personalized Value Statements:**
   "Reflecting on our last discussion about your current challenges with [specific issue], I believe our solution could not only address these pain points but also create growth opportunities. Let's explore how this aligns with your strategic objectives."

4. **Visual and Interactive Content:**
   "Attached is an infographic that outlines the step-by-step impact our services have had on similar organizations. I think you'll find it illustrates the value clearly and

engagingly."

5. **Future-Oriented Messaging:**
   "Investing in our solution today means setting your organization up for success in the future. By enhancing your capabilities now, you're preparing your team to meet the challenges and opportunities of tomorrow."

By consistently highlighting how your offering transforms organizational outcomes, you not only reinforce the value but also build a compelling case that resonates with potential customers. This approach shifts the focus from a simple transaction to a strategic partnership, paving the way for long-term loyalty and mutual success.

Let me take you back to 2002—a time when many small business owners stuck to cash or checks. I was in the credit card processing business, and I met a memorable owner of a bustling wing restaurant in Memphis. Picture an accountant running a popular wing joint, entirely convinced that accepting credit cards would cost him 2-5% of his hard-earned profits. He was so determined to avoid that fee that he even toyed with the idea of installing an ATM right in his restaurant, so customers would have to pay in cash!

Instead of bombarding him with sales jargon or pressuring him to change his mind, I decided to share a story and ask a few thoughtful questions. I explained, with genuine enthusiasm, that while a 2-5% fee might look like a setback at first, there was a much bigger picture to consider. When customers pay with a card, they often end up spending more—and that extra spending could easily cover the fee and then some. I painted a picture of how accepting all forms of payment could open up new revenue streams and create a smoother, more inviting customer experience.

I could see his skepticism slowly give way to curiosity, and then—lightbulb moment—he began to see that accepting credit cards wasn't just an expense. It was an investment in his business's future, a way to boost sales and keep up with the evolving market.

You don't build a business—you build
people, and then people build the business."
— Zig Ziglar.

This experience taught me a valuable lesson: when you remind potential customers of the real, lasting impact on their organization, you help them see beyond immediate costs. It's about sharing a vision of growth and opportunity, and building trust through genuine, heartfelt conversation. When you speak with passion and share your story, customers start to see the actual value of what you offer—and that's when lasting relationships are born.

CHAPTER 6

Persuasion Through Service

Let's be honest—"persuasion" has gotten a bad rap. When people hear the word, they think manipulation. Pressure. Slick talkers who will say anything to close a deal.

But factual persuasion—servant-based persuasion—isn't about pushing someone into a yes. It's about helping them come to it on their own, because they trust you, believe in the value you bring, and feel safe moving forward.

That's not manipulation. That's leadership.

And the best leaders? They persuade by serving.

The Power of Influence, Not Pressure

If you want to be persuasive in business—or in life—you've got to drop the idea that power comes from control. Real power comes from influence, and influence is earned through service.

People don't change because you convince them.
People change because they feel seen, understood, and supported.

That's the new persuasion.

> *"Let each of you look not only to his own interests, but also to the interests of others."*
> *— Philippians 2:4*

What Servant-Based Persuasion Looks Like

Here's what persuasion through service actually looks like in action:

- You ask more questions than you answer.

- You guide instead of pushing.

- You listen to understand—not to respond.

- You share what's possible—not what's pressured.

- You talk less.

Think of it like a doctor. The best doctors don't just say, "Here, take this." They examine, ask questions, explain, and involve you in the process. They help you say yes to the solution, because you trust the diagnosis.

Sales is no different.

3 Questions to Guide Servant-Based Persuasion

Before you try to "persuade" anyone of anything, ask yourself:

1. Is what I'm offering truly in their best interest?

2. Am I listening more than I'm speaking?

3. Would I want someone to approach me this way?

If you can answer yes, you're persuading with integrity. If not, you're selling for self, not service.

Real-World Example: Serving Over Selling in Merchant Services

I once met with a small business owner—let's call him James. He was skeptical about switching to our payment solution. Another rep had pitched him before.

Instead of diving into numbers, I started with questions:

"What's your biggest frustration with your current system?"

"How much time are you spending on this each week?"

"If we could make one thing easier, what would it be?"

Ten minutes in, he wasn't listening to a pitch; he was being heard. And because I listened, I was able to connect my solution to his needs, not just my offer.

He didn't just sign the deal. He thanked me for caring enough to ask.

Sales isn't about pushing products—it's about positioning solutions.

Let's start with a clear picture: imagine Michael Jordan Brand sneakers. No commercials. No hard sell. No countdown emails. Just a quiet announcement: "The drop is Saturday," and then the product is gone. Sold out. Lines wrapped around the block. Why? Because they've built buying power. Years of delivering quality, building culture, and staying consistent. They've served their audience so well that they no longer need to pitch. The demand is already there.

Same with Chick-fil-A. Is it the best chicken sandwich in the world? That's debatable. But you know what *isn't* debatable? The experience. The consistency. The feeling that you're going to be served with care every single time. We pull into that drive-thru because we already know what we're getting. That's buying power.

And that's the problem with most entrepreneurs: they're pitching before they've positioned. They're chasing sales before they've served. They're begging for attention before they've built trust.

And then they wonder why the conversion rate is low or the launch flopped.

When you lead with service, you're not just building goodwill; you're creating what I call buying power—the internal readiness in a person to say yes before the offer is even made.

And here's the deeper layer: **buy-in power creates buying power**.

When people are emotionally, mentally, or spiritually bought into your mission, your message, and your movement, they're much more likely to say yes with their money. Buy-in comes from how you serve, how you show up, and how you stay consistent. It's the trust tax they're willing to pay because they believe in *you*.

Just like people line up for Jordan drops or stick with Chick-fil-A despite competition, it's not always about the product—it's about the **position**. It's about the story, the standard, and the sense of trust. That's buy-in power. And it leads to buying power. The fundamental persuasion framework is expressed in the way they care.

The Framework: Persuade with C.A.R.E.

Here's a simple way to remember how to lead with service in every conversation:

C.A.R.E.	WHAT IT MEANS	HOW TO USE IT
C – Connect Personally	Build rapport and make it relational, not transactional.	Start with shared interests, compliments, or empathy.
A – Ask with Purpose	Get curious about their pain points, desires, and concerns.	Ask open-ended, thoughtful questions.
R – Recommend with Integrity	Only recommend what serves their best outcome.	Align your offer with their stated goals—not your sales quota.
E – Empower the Decision	Don't pressure—equip them to choose.	Offer clarity, confidence, and control. Let them lead the yes.

How Jesus Persuaded Without Pressure

Let's not forget the ultimate servant leader: Jesus. He persuaded crowds, transformed lives, and started a movement that's still growing 2,000 years later. But he never pressured anyone.

He served. He listened. He met people where they were. And He always left room for free will.

In sales, we often forget that giving people the power to choose is the most persuasive move of all.

Don't Push—Pull

Pushy salespeople chase people away. Servant sellers draw people in. Because people don't want to be convinced—they want to be cared for.

So the next time you're in a conversation, don't think about what you want to say. Think about what they need to hear. And most of the time? That starts with listening.

Reflection Questions:

- Am I persuading people, or pressuring them?

- Have I been serving with my words, or just selling with them?

- What would it look like to put more "care" into my conversations?

CHAPTER 7

Serving Smarter with AI

"The best way to predict the future is to create it." — Peter Drucker

Artificial intelligence is no longer a concept of the future—it's a tool of the present. But here's the truth: AI doesn't replace people, it empowers them. It doesn't remove relationships; it enhances them. Used wisely, AI gives us back the most valuable resource of all *time*. Time to serve better, listen longer, and show up more prepared.

The New Tool in Our Hands

When I first started in sales, my "AI" was a yellow legal pad and a box of index cards. I'd write down customer names, their kids' birthdays, what they bought, and little details that made them feel remembered. I had to handwrite follow-ups, call reminders, and stack folders on my desk like skyscrapers. It worked—but it was slow, clunky, and often out of date before I could even flip to the next card.

Fast-forward to today. AI can instantly pull customer histories, summarize call transcripts, suggest next steps, and even build personalized outreach scripts in seconds. What once took hours now takes minutes.

But one thing hasn't changed—the mission.
The goal isn't just to sell faster; it's to serve deeper. The tool just got sharper.

Yesterday vs. Today: A Real-Time Comparison

TASK	YESTERDAY (MANUAL EFFORT)	TODAY (WITH AI ASSISTANCE)
Preparing for a client meeting	2–3 hours of research, reading notes, printing reports	10–15 minutes for AI to summarize the client's updates, extract trends, and highlight opportunities
Writing follow-up emails	20–30 minutes each, per customer	2–3 minutes—AI drafts an outline, and you personalize it
Brainstorming scripts or discovery questions	Trial and error, often recycled from old presentations	Instant tailored prompts for each vertical and personality type
Tracking performance insights	Manual spreadsheets, delayed reports	Real-time dashboards powered by predictive data
Reviewing a proposal	Multiple revisions and rewrites	AI edits for clarity, tone, and accuracy before you hit send

How AI Enhances Scripts and Conversations

Let's be honest—most salespeople lose confidence in the first 30 seconds. The wrong opener, a flat delivery, or a missed question can kill momentum. AI can help you turn hesitation into preparation.

Here's how:

- **Customized Openers:** Drafts intros that match your customer's communication style—formal or conversational.

- **Objection Role-Plays:** Simulates real scenarios so you can practice and refine responses.

- **Insight-Driven Questions:** Generates prompts rooted in current industry trends.

For instance, instead of the tired line: *"Hi, I'd like to tell you about our services."*
AI might suggest: *"I noticed many healthcare leaders are struggling to streamline communication between multiple sites—how has that been affecting your team lately?"*

The difference? One is a pitch. The other is a partnership.

AI helps you walk into a meeting prepared to listen, not just talk. It allows you to anticipate pain points and enter every conversation from a place of service rather than pressure.

Using AI to Understand Verticals

One of the most innovative ways to use AI is to study *verticals*—specific industries or customer segments. AI can digest massive amounts of data that would take you weeks to sort through. And it can help you speak your client's language fluently.

- **Healthcare:** AI can analyze turnover rates, compliance changes, or patient-care bottlenecks. You can walk into meetings already knowing what's keeping them up at night.

- **Construction:** It can flag material cost fluctuations, project delays, or workforce shortages. That insight lets you position your solution as timely and relevant.

- **Telecom & Technology:** AI tracks bandwidth spikes, connectivity trends, or remote-work expansion, helping you present solutions before the customer even asks.

- **Real Estate:** It can evaluate local inventory cycles, mortgage trends, and pricing behaviors, allowing you to connect emotionally and financially.

When you show up informed, customers see more than a salesperson—they see a consultant, a partner, and in many cases, a trusted advisor.

The Human Advantage in the Age of AI

Artificial intelligence can process information, but only spiritual intelligence can process intention.
AI can tell you what's happening, but not *why* it matters. It can track sentiment, but not sincerity.

That's where *you* come in.

AI can't feel compassion, conviction, or calling—but you can. Empathy isn't a "soft skill"; it's a competitive advantage. When you slow down enough to truly listen—to catch the hesitation in a client's voice, the pause before they answer, or the joy when they talk about their team—you're hearing what no algorithm can detect.

True sales mastery now lies at the intersection of **discernment and data**. I call it a *Spirit-led strategy*—where you let wisdom lead, and AI assist.

AI may tell you the customer's buying history, but your inner spirit will reveal the customer's heart.

Use both. That's how you win with integrity and impact.

Proverbs 4:7 says, "Wisdom is the principal thing; therefore get wisdom: and with all thy getting get understanding."

AI delivers information, but only wisdom delivers impact.

- Wisdom reminds you not to let technology talk louder than your testimony.

- Wisdom tells you that data is powerful, but discernment is priceless.

- Wisdom teaches that speed means nothing if sincerity is missing.

AI can write a script, but only you can live the story.

Ethics, Privacy, and Trust

Technology can be fast, but trust takes time—and ethics are the bridge between the two.

Tell your clients openly:

"I use AI tools to serve you better—not to sell you."

Transparency builds credibility. And credibility builds loyalty.

If you're using AI to summarize a meeting or analyze notes, always remove private financial or sensitive details. Don't just protect data; protect dignity.

"Whoever can be trusted with very little can also be trusted with much." — *Luke 16:10*

AI can't fix a character flaw. Technology only multiplies what's already in your heart.

When Technology Meets Testimony

AI may prepare your notes, but the Spirit prepares your heart.

I remember a morning before a big presentation to a national client. I had used AI to gather every fact, trend, and data point about their business. But before I left the office, I prayed: "Lord, show me how to serve this client beyond the numbers."

During the meeting, I felt prompted to pause and ask a question not in my notes:
"How's your team holding up with all this growth?"

The room shifted. The CEO exhaled and said, "Honestly, morale has been rough." That one question changed everything. We talked about people before products, purpose before price.

AI helped me prepare, but wisdom helped me connect.
When technology meets testimony, results follow—because people don't just buy what you know, they buy how you care.

AI in Daily Sales Leadership

AI isn't just for individuals—it can revolutionize how leaders serve their teams.

Here's how you can use it daily:

- **Pipeline Reviews:** Let AI summarize deal stages and highlight stalled accounts so your one-on-ones can focus on coaching, not numbers.

- **Team Insights:** Identify patterns—who's best at follow-ups, who needs help managing objections, who's building the most trust.

- **Territory Planning:** Predict trends before they appear and adjust strategy accordingly.

- **Coaching Moments:** Use AI summaries of client feedback to personalize development plans.

When you lead this way, your meetings shift from pressure sessions to growth sessions. You're not chasing performance—you're cultivating purpose.

A real leader doesn't just read reports—they read people.

Preparing for What's Next

AI isn't slowing down. Soon, we'll see tools that can build meeting summaries in real time, and suggest next steps before the conversation even ends.

But even in that future, your humanity remains the differentiator.

Robots won't run the future. It'll be led by servants who know how to use them.

Adaptability is now a spiritual discipline. As Romans 12:2 says: *"Be transformed by the renewing of your mind."*

Stay teachable. Stay curious. Stay grounded in your purpose.

Leaders who serve with humility and learn with hunger will thrive—not because they mastered technology, but because they never stopped mastering themselves.

Reflection Questions

1. How am I preparing for customer conversations—and could AI help me prepare deeper, not just faster?

2. Am I using technology to connect or to hide?

3. Where can I reinvest the time AI saves me—into people, purpose, or personal growth?

4. Do my words sound like service, or like sales?

AI isn't the future—it's the *now*.
But here's the truth: tools don't create trust. People do.

When you stop selling and start serving, AI becomes your assistant, not your replacement. It sharpens your preparation, strengthens your communication, and gives you the breathing room to lead with empathy and excellence.

Whether you're holding a legal pad, a smartphone, or the latest AI software, one principle remains the same: *serve first, and sales will follow.*

So keep serving. Keep learning. Keep showing up prepared—heart first, data second.

CHAPTER 8

Cultivating a Servant Leadership Culture in Sales

If you're in a leadership role, your ability to serve impacts your entire team's success. A servant leadership culture in sales isn't about pushing people to meet quotas—it's about equipping, empowering, and guiding them toward success.

Here's how you cultivate it:

1. Training and Development Programs

- Invest in skills training—not just on sales techniques, but on problem-solving, emotional intelligence, and relationship-building.

- Encourage ongoing learning through books, podcasts, and mentorship.

- Teach service-based selling, where the focus is on understanding and solving customer needs, not just closing deals.

2. Creating a Supportive and Collaborative Environment

- Foster a culture where team members help each other, rather than compete against one another.

- Celebrate wins collectively, reinforcing that success is a team effort.

- Provide open communication channels where employees feel heard and valued.

3. Mentoring and Coaching Team Members

- Lead by example—show your team what it looks like to serve, don't just tell them.

- Pair experienced team members with newer ones for mentorship.

- Have one-on-one coaching sessions to understand individual strengths and challenges.

Success Story: Leading Teams at Comcast Business

When I was a sales leader in Memphis and Pennsylvania at Comcast Business, I had the privilege and responsibility of leading sales teams. Through that experience, I learned an important truth:

"Lead people collectively. Know them individually."

What does that mean? Leading collectively means:

- Everyone on the team must have a shared vision and a common goal.

- We are all working toward the same mission and results.

However, how we get there is unique to each team member. Every salesperson has different strengths, personalities, and talents:

- Some were great at cold calling and working the phones.

- Others excelled in face-to-face meetings and building relationships in person.

- Some thrived at networking events (which happens to be my personal favorite).

- Others were just naturally good at connecting with people on a personal level.

The key to effective leadership was recognizing these differences and allowing each team member to lean into their strengths. Instead of forcing a one-size-fits-all approach, I encouraged them to use their unique abilities while still working toward the collective mission.

And what happened?

- Our team performed better.

- Morale was higher.

- People felt valued, supported, and empowered.

Why? Because when you serve your team, they, in turn, serve their customers better. And when customers feel served, sales naturally follow.

One Moment That Opened My Eyes

Back when I was leading sales teams at Comcast Business, I noticed something that completely changed how I viewed sales. Some of my best salespeople weren't necessarily the ones making the most calls or setting the most meetings. Instead, they were the ones who took the time to listen, understand, and solve their clients' problems.

One name stands out when I think about this: Cindy.

When Cindy came on board at Comcast, she didn't have a traditional sales background. She was a business owner, not a career salesperson. But what she did have was a deep understanding of what it meant to serve people.

Unlike many sales reps who passed off customer issues to someone else or treated service problems as "not their job," Cindy took a different approach. She didn't just sell—she helped.

If a customer had a problem, she didn't brush them off or send them through a maze of corporate channels. She stayed with them, worked through their issues, and made sure they got the resolution they needed.

And what happened? She became the top salesperson in Business Sales for years—consistently exceeding quota year after year.

But even more importantly, her customers became loyal to her. They weren't just buying a product or a service; they were investing in a relationship with someone they trusted—someone who served first and sold second.

Cindy's story is proof that serving, not selling, is what creates long-term success. She didn't win because she had the best pitch or the most aggressive sales tactics. She won because she genuinely cared, and that care turned into trust, loyalty, and results that spoke for themselves.

That lesson stuck with me. The best salespeople aren't the ones who chase numbers. They're the ones who build relationships. And you build relationships by serving first.

CHAPTER 9

Measuring and Celebrating Team Achievements

CHAPTER 9 - MEASURING AND CELEBRATING TEAM ACHIEVEMENTS

Most companies have a rewards program to recognize their top salespeople. Some call it "President's Club," others call it "Winner's Circle," and some even have names like "Legends Club" or "Summit Elite." These awards come with luxury trips, big bonuses, and serious recognition. And don't get me wrong—they're great.

But here's what I've learned: winning starts long before the big trip. It begins with the small achievements—the moments when you push a little harder, help one more customer, and focus on serving rather than selling.

I've been blessed to win a few of these trips in my career. And let me tell you, they were unforgettable.

The Cancun Charter Plane—Like a Rockstar!

One of my first big trips was to Cancun when I worked for an ADT Authorized Dealer. But this wasn't just any trip; we flew on a private chartered plane. That's right, no security lines, no crowded terminals—just straight VIP treatment.

I remember stepping onto that plane, looking around, and thinking, "Man, is this real life?" The energy was electric: people laughing, music playing, drinks flowing before we even left the ground. We weren't just going on vacation; we were being celebrated.

Then there was Maui. This was next level. My wife, Catrina, and I won an all-expenses-paid trip to Hawaii through the merchant services company I worked for in Houston. But this wasn't just a trip; it was an experience.

We stayed at the Ritz-Carlton. And if you've ever been to a Ritz, you already know, it's a whole different world. The kind where you don't carry your own bags, the staff knows your name, and they make you feel like royalty.

To top it all off, they gave us $500 cash for incidentals. Yes—$500 to spend however we wanted.

But the most breathtaking part of the trip wasn't the hotel, the beaches, or even the luxury—it was the night sky.

I remember walking outside at night, looking up, and being stunned. The stars—they looked so close, I felt like I could reach up and grab one. It was a reminder of how big the world is and how limitless the possibilities are.

And here's the craziest part: I never set my sights on winning either of those trips.

I wasn't tracking my sales every day, sweating the leaderboard, or obsessing over quotas. In fact, I didn't even realize I was in the running until I was told right before the qualifying period ended.

So what's my point?

When your focus isn't on YOU, things happen FOR you.

I wasn't chasing a prize—I was serving customers, doing the work, and trying to be the best version of myself. And because of that, the rewards followed.

Lessons from the Wins

So, what did I take away from these experiences?

1. Focus on service, not the scoreboard. When you help others, your success becomes a byproduct of your actions.

2. Celebrate small wins. The big rewards come from consistently doing the small things right.

3. Unexpected blessings come when you're not chasing them. When you focus on the work, God, the universe, or

whatever you believe in, it aligns things in your favor.

These trips were incredible. The luxury, the experiences, the VIP treatment—all of it was amazing. But what made them truly special was realizing that serving first always leads to rewards bigger than you ever expected.

So, if you're grinding right now, putting in the work, wondering if anyone even notices, keep going.

Because one day, when you least expect it, someone's gonna tap you on the shoulder and tell you, "Pack your bags—you're going to paradise."

> *"Don't worry about being successful, but work toward being significant, and the success will naturally follow."*
>
> *— Oprah Winfrey*

CHAPTER 10

Learn From Others

One of the most important truths I've learned in life is this:

You don't have to go through everything to grow through something.

~Les Brown

Too many people try to figure everything out on their own. They waste years bumping their heads against the same walls someone else already knocked down. But growth doesn't have to be lonely. The most intelligent people I know don't just have drive; they have *guidance*.

That's why I'm a student before I'm a leader. A listener before I'm a teacher. A servant before I'm a seller.

Because the truth is: **you can't lead well if you don't learn well.**

Wisdom is Everywhere—If You're Open to It

Some of my most life-changing lessons didn't come from business books or boardrooms. They came from barbershops. From church pews. From mentors who didn't even know they were mentoring me.

It came from Vernon, the man who told me:

> "Son, when you start looking professional, you start acting professional. And soon, you become that professional person."

That one sentence shifted my entire mindset. I started dressing, walking, and talking differently. And before long, I began closing deals differently.

It didn't happen overnight. But it started because I was *willing to learn.*

It's Not a Pitch, It's a Conversation

Too many people approach sales like a performance. They rehearse their lines, deliver their points, and hope the audience applauds with their wallets. But sales isn't theatre. It's not about getting someone to say yes on command. It's about connection, clarity, and trust.

That's why the most powerful sales happen in conversation—not in presentation.

When you talk with someone instead of at them, you give them room to think, to process, and most importantly, to trust you. You aren't pressuring them into a decision—you're guiding them toward a solution.

Let me tell you about someone who embodied this idea better than most: Dr. Randal Pinkett. I had the pleasure of meeting and speaking with Dr. Pinkett at a conference in Philadelphia, where his presence off stage was just as impactful as his platform message. We talked briefly about legacy, leadership, and the weight of standing in your truth—something he knows a lot about.

Randal was a contestant on *The Apprentice*. He won the season. In addition to completing tasks well, he earned the respect of Donald Trump and the nation that was watching. But what stood out most wasn't his resume—it was his restraint.

At the end of the season, after weeks of competition, Trump asked Randal if he should hire the runner-up as well. Cameras rolling. Pressure high. This was a moment that could've been a soft PR move.

But Randal didn't play to the crowd. He said respectfully, "There can only be one Apprentice." That wasn't arrogance. That was conviction. Clarity. Leadership.

He knew what he brought to the table. He wasn't afraid to stand firm—not to tear others down, but to uphold his own worth.

That's what a real sales conversation sounds like. Not pushy. Not flashy. Just clear.

When you know the value of what you offer, you don't overcompensate with noise. You speak with purpose. You invite questions. You build dialogue.

Just like Nike's Jordan brand doesn't need a commercial every time a shoe drops… just like Chick-fil-A doesn't need to shout for attention…

The brands—and people—that lead the best conversations are the ones who already did the real work: serving first, standing firm, and showing up consistently.

Remember this: you don't need to pitch hard when you're already trusted. You need to show up with confidence, clarity, and care.

That's the conversation that converts.

Randel Pinkett at a leadership conference in Philadelphia, PA

Learning from Giants: Mentors Who Changed My Life

Let me give you a few names and the one thing each of them taught me. If you're serious about growth, I recommend you study them, too.

MENTOR	SIGNATURE LESSON
Les Brown	"When life knocks you down, try to land on your back. Because if you can look up, you can get up."
Myron Golden	Money follows value. The best sellers solve the biggest problems."
Eric Thomas	"Don't cry to give up; cry to keep going."
Lisa Nichols	"Your current situation is not your final destination. Speak life, even when life feels silent."
Jim Rohn	"Work harder on yourself than you do on your job." Personal development is the key to professional success.
Stephen Covey	"Begin with the end in mind." Clarity fuels impact.
Booker T. Washington	"If you want to lift yourself, lift someone else." Service creates significance.

Vernon Johnson and the Day Everything Changed

Back when I was working as a bail bondsman—what I liked to call a *"freedom salesman"*—I found myself in one of the most unpredictable and humbling chapters of my life.

Let me paint the picture for you.

I was showing up every day to the courthouse in Memphis, helping families post bail for their loved ones. It wasn't glamorous. Some days were chaotic, others heartbreaking. I saw people at their lowest: scared, angry, desperate. But I was there to serve. To give folks a second chance. To get them back home.

But even while I was handling business, I didn't feel like a businessman.

I'd wear whatever I could throw on quickly. My confidence? Shaky. I was still trying to figure out what kind of man I was becoming—and whether I even *belonged* in the world of professionals.

Then one day, I noticed a man who stood out from the crowd like a spotlight in the dark.

His name? Vernon Johnson.

Slim build. Sharp suit. Polished shoes. The way he walked through the courthouse? Smooth. Confident. Like he owned the air around him. I watched him from a distance for weeks, wondering if he was a lawyer or maybe even a judge. He had *that* kind of energy. The kind that made you want to sit up straighter when he walked by.

Finally, I got up the nerve to ask him, "Excuse me, sir... are you an attorney?"

He smiled. "No, I'm not."

"Well," I asked, "how do you carry yourself like that? How do you show up so sharp, so professional—like you were made for this place?"

He paused. Then he looked me square in the eyes. That's when he said the quote I mentioned earlier. A statement I pray I never forget:

"Son, when you start looking professional, you start acting professional. And soon, you become that professional person."

That one sentence flipped a switch in me.

The Shift That Started with a Suit

After that encounter, I changed how I walked into the building.

I upgraded my wardrobe—not because I wanted to impress people, but because I needed to remind *myself* who I was becoming. I started standing taller, speaking clearly, and showing up earlier.

My confidence grew. No, the world didn't suddenly change. *I* did.

And it all started with Vernon Johnson—a man who didn't have to say much, but whose presence taught me everything.

That's the power of example. That's the power of mentorship—even when it's quiet.

Looking back now, I realize Vernon taught me more than how to dress. He taught me the value of *aligning with my identity*.

If you want to become a high performer, a servant leader, a trusted voice in your field, you've got to *see* yourself that way before others do.

The suit didn't make me who I am.
 But it reminded me of who I was becoming.

Learn Loud, Practice Quiet

Learning isn't just about consumption. It's about the application.

- You can watch every video.

- Read every book.

- Quote every speaker.

But if you don't live it, it's just noise.

The people who grow are the ones who *do the work*. They take what they've learned and apply it to their business, their conversations, and their service.

If Les says, "You gotta be hungry," and you're still hitting snooze—you didn't learn it.

If Myron says, "Sell the result, not the product," and you're still pitching features—you didn't learn it.

> *Learning is a lifestyle. Not a weekend hobby.*

How to Stay Motivated When the Journey Gets Long

The business of sales is a rollercoaster. One minute you're up. Next, you're wondering if you even belong in the industry.

Here's what's helped me stay grounded:

1. **Fuel Your Mind Daily**

   o Podcasts, sermons, audiobooks—every day.

   o What you feed your mind will eventually come out of your mouth.

2. **Get Around Hungry People**

- Your environment will either stretch you or shrink you.

- Be around folks who are going *somewhere*.

Track Your Growth

- Not just your sales, but your habits.

- Ask yourself weekly: What did I learn? What did I apply?

3. **Take Breaks Without Breaking Down**

- Rest is part of the journey. Don't feel guilty for recharging.

A Note to the Learner-Leader

You don't need to know everything. You need to be teachable because teachability will take you further than talent ever will.

And here's the truth most people won't tell you:

The day you stop learning is the day you stop leading.

You want to build a business that lasts? A team that thrives? A career that brings purpose?

Then keep learning. Keep stretching. Keep seeking wisdom.

Reflection Questions:

- Who are the three voices I'm learning from right now— and how are they shaping me?

- What lesson have I *heard* but not yet *applied?*

- Am I more interested in looking smart—or actually growing wise?

The Importance of Ongoing Learning and Self-Improvement

Success isn't a one-time event—it's a lifelong journey. You don't just wake up one day and say, "I've made it." No matter how much you accomplish, **there's always another level to reach.** The people who continuously grow are the ones who constantly seek knowledge and new perspectives.

I've learned from incredible mentors, both directly and from afar. But three voices in particular have impacted me the most: **Les Brown, Myron Golden, and Eric Thomas.**

- **Les Brown** taught me the power of belief—he always says, *"You gotta be hungry!"* Success doesn't come to the passive. It comes to those who **relentlessly pursue** their goals.

- **Myron Golden** showed me that selling isn't just about making money—it's about solving problems and serving people. He emphasizes how wealth follows those who create value.

- **Eric Thomas (ET the Hip Hop Preacher)** reminds me to **outwork everyone in the room.** He says, *"When you want to succeed as bad as you want to breathe, then you'll be successful."* That mindset of **grit, perseverance, and hunger** separates the greats from the rest.

I've taken bits and pieces from each of these mentors and applied them to my own life. **That's the key—learning from others and using their wisdom to elevate yourself.**

Myron Golden's Studio Tampa, FL

Les Brown Keynote Speaker Memphis, TN

How to Stay Motivated and Inspired in Sales

Let's be honest: **sales can be tough.** You face rejection, uncertainty, and sometimes, it feels like nothing is going your way. But staying motivated is what separates the ones who make it from those who quit too soon. Here's what works for me:

1. **Constantly Feed Your Mind** – Listen to audiobooks, watch motivational videos, and read daily. **What you put in your mind shapes your thoughts, and your thoughts shape your results.**

2. **Set Goals That Stretch You** – If your goals don't challenge you, they won't change you. Aim higher than you think is possible.

3. **Surround Yourself with Winners – Your environment influences your energy.** If you spend time around people who complain, you'll complain. If you spend time with people who push themselves, you'll push yourself.

4. **Celebrate Small Wins** – Progress keeps you going. Every deal, every new relationship, every lesson learned is a step forward.

5. **Serve, Don't Sell** – When you focus on helping people, your motivation naturally increases because your work has purpose.

The Role of Continuous Feedback and Adaptation

One of the biggest lessons I've learned is that **growth requires feedback.** If you want to get better, you have to be willing to hear the truth—even when it stings.

- **Listen to your customers.** If they hesitate or push back, figure out why. Don't get defensive—get better.

- **Review your own performance.** If a deal didn't close, ask yourself, *"What could I have done differently?"*

- **Seek mentorship and coaching.** Great athletes have coaches. Great businesspeople have mentors. If you want to win, you need someone who can see your blind spots and push you to the next level.

-

The Importance of Ongoing Learning and Self-Improvement

Success isn't a one-time event—it's a **lifelong journey**. No matter how much you accomplish, **there's always another level to reach.** The people who continuously grow are the ones who **actively seek knowledge, push their limits, and embrace self-improvement.**

The Story of Lisa Nichols: From Food Stamps to World-Renowned Speaker

Lisa Nichols' journey is one of the most inspiring examples of self-improvement and relentless perseverance. She was a single mother, living on food stamps, with only $11.42 in her bank account. At one point, she had to wrap her son in a towel because she couldn't afford diapers. She hit rock bottom.

But she made a decision—a decision that she would not let her current situation define her future. She invested in herself, devoured books, attended seminars, and trained her mind to see possibility instead of limitation.

Fast forward to today, and Lisa Nichols is a world-renowned speaker, best-selling author, and millionaire entrepreneur. She has inspired millions of people with her story, proving that where you start does not determine where you finish.

One of my favorite Lisa Nichols quotes is:

> *"Your greatest fear is not that you are inadequate. Your greatest fear is that you are powerful beyond measure."*

Lisa's transformation was not overnight—it was the result of consistent learning, self-discipline, and the decision never to stop growing.

**Lisa Nichols Speak & Write
Conference (San Diego, CA)**

Learning is the Key to Growth

The lesson is simple: **If you want to achieve more, you have to become more.**

I've seen it in my own life. Every major breakthrough I've had—whether in sales, leadership, or personal success—came from:

✅ Reading, studying, and learning from those who've done it before me.

✅ Seeking out mentors and applying their wisdom.

✅ Pushing myself beyond my comfort zone, even when it felt uncomfortable.

Success leaves clues. Lisa Nichols, Les Brown, Myron Golden, Eric Thomas, and Jim Rohn all started at the bottom, but they committed to ongoing learning and self-improvement—and that changed everything.

If you're reading this, let me remind you: **your situation today does not define your future.** Keep learning. Keep growing. **You are powerful beyond measure.**

CHAPTER **11**

From Unaware to Advocate —
Serving Every Step of the Way

"People don't buy when they understand you. They buy when they feel understood."
— Melvin White.

Every great business story begins in the same place: obscurity. No one knows your name, your product, or your purpose. But then comes that first spark—an introduction, a conversation, a moment of connection. From that point on, the relationship either grows or fades depending on how you show up.

Most people think marketing is about being seen. But authentic leadership is about seeing others first. It's about recognizing the person behind the purchase and the story behind the sale. The shift from unaware to advocate isn't a transaction—it's a transformation.

This chapter is about that transformation. It's about the invisible bridge that turns strangers into supporters and customers into champions. It's the path of empathy, listening, and consistent service—the kind that builds trust, not pressure; relationships, not revenue goals.

Because when people feel understood, they stop being customers. They become your community.

Every customer is on a journey—from not knowing you exist to becoming your most prominent advocate.
Most salespeople try to "close the deal," but servant leaders build relationships. Because the truth is, *sales isn't a finish line—it's a trust line.*

When you lead with service at every step, you don't just gain customers—you gain partners, friends, and ambassadors for your mission.

Stage 1: Awareness — They Don't Know You Yet

At this stage, people aren't looking for you. They're busy living life, managing problems you're equipped to solve—if they only knew you existed.

Serve, Don't Sell Moves:

1. **Educate before you advertise.** Post tips, record short videos, and write articles that solve problems freely. Value earns visibility.
2. **Show up where they are.** Join their world before inviting them into yours. Comment, encourage, and engage without selling.

3. **Tell relatable stories.** People connect with stories that mirror their own struggles. Share transformation, not transactions.

Do: "Hey, I saw your post about struggling with inventory. Here's a checklist I built that might help."
Don't: "We offer a great system for that—want a demo?"

Stage 2: Consideration — They're Curious, Not Convinced

Now they know who you are—but they're testing if they can trust you.
This is where most sellers push. But servants pause.

Serve, Don't Sell Moves:

1. **Ask before you advise.** "What's most important to you in fixing this?"
2. **Share evidence, not ego.** Use success stories, reviews, or results to validate without boasting.
3. **Respect their pace.** Consistency builds comfort; pressure destroys it.

Do: "I'd love to walk through what success might look like for your team."
Don't: "Just checking in to see if you've made a decision yet."

Stage 3: Decision — Help, Don't Hustle

This is where buyers either lean in—or pull back. And your tone determines which one it is.

Serve, Don't Sell Moves:

1. **Clarify the value, not the price.** Help them see what they *gain* and what they *lose* by doing nothing.
2. **Offer choices, not ultimatums.** Good–Better–Best options empower, they don't pressure.
3. **Make the next step safe.** Guarantees, trial periods, or low-risk pilots show confidence and care.

Do: "Here are three levels of partnership depending on where you'd like to start."
Don't: "This deal expires at midnight."

Packaging Value in Tiers: The Good–Better–Best Framework

In my business, I teach this model because it honors both the buyer's confidence and their capacity.

- **Good:** The essentials—solves the core problem.
- **Better:** Adds comfort, convenience, or support.
- **Best:** Creates transformation and long-term impact.

Anchor wisely: Start with *Best* to show the whole vision, then step down as needed.
Guarantee with integrity: A guarantee should remove fear, not manipulate urgency.

"If this doesn't bring measurable value in 30 days, I'll make it right."

The Cost of Doing Nothing—Without Pressure:

"You don't have to decide today. I want you to weigh the real cost of staying where you are—lost time, missed opportunity, and delayed progress. My goal is clarity, not a quick close."

When you approach the decision moment like this, people don't feel cornered—they feel cared for.

Stage 3½ | Handling Objections Without Getting Slimy

"If you have to push, you're not aligned.
Pressure is proof you've stopped serving."
— Melvin White.

Objections aren't rejection; they're reflection. They expose fears, not foes.

The Memphis Restaurant Story

A restaurant owner refused to take credit cards: "I'm not paying 3 percent to a bank."
I asked, "How many walk out because you don't take cards?"
When we did the math, he saw he was losing thousands to save hundreds.

He didn't need a pitch—he required perspective.
Clarity closes what pressure never could.

The A-P-R-D Framework

1. **Ask:** "I get that. Can I ask what's giving you pause?"
2. **Probe:** "Is it timing, budget, or something I didn't explain clearly?"
3. **Reframe:** "Some clients felt the same way until they saw the real risk was in waiting."
4. **Decide:** "Whether you move now or later, I want this decision to feel right."

Real-World Dialogues

Price Objection

Customer: "It's too expensive."
Me: "Totally fair. Can I ask what you're comparing it to?"

Customer: "Just didn't expect the cost."
Me: "If it saves five hours a week at $50 an hour, that's $1,000 a month. Would investing $300 to gain $1,000 sound reasonable?"

That's not pressure—it's perspective.

Trust Objection

"I understand. Let's slow down the sale and speed up the trust. We'll start small, and if you're not satisfied in 30 days, I'll make it right myself."

Trust is built when people feel safe to say *maybe*.

The Cindy Belk Lesson

Cindy didn't "overcome" objections—she *walked through* them. When a customer worried about switching providers, she said,

"Here's my number. I'll personally call you the first week to make sure everything's smooth." That care turned a hesitation into a long-term relationship.

Objection Quick-Guide

OBJECTION	DON'T SAY THIS	DO SAY THIS
PRICE	"It's not that expensive."	"Let's compare the return, not just the cost."
TIMING	"This deal expires tonight."	"What would make the timing feel right for you?"
TOUCH	"We've been around for 20 years."	"Would you like to speak with a client who was in your same position?"

Stage 4: Onboarding — The Vulnerable First 30 Days

The sale is made—but trust is still fragile.
This is the moment to reinforce why they said yes.

Serve, Don't Sell Moves:

1. **Celebrate their decision.** Send a thank-you note or a voice message to express your appreciation for their trust.
2. **Create a 30–60–90 Day Plan.** Define goals, milestones, and roles.
3. **Deliver a quick win.** Help them experience an early success they can feel.

Kickoff Call Checklist:
Review goals and success criteria.
Confirm who does what by when
Set a first milestone call.
Celebrate the partnership

Do: "Here's what your first 90 days will look like—together."
Don't: "We'll get started soon."

Stage 5: Adoption — Building Confidence Through Use

Now they're using your product or service. This is where belief becomes behavior.

Serve, Don't Sell Moves:

1. **Check in without an ask.** "How's it working for you so far?"
2. **Educate continuously.** Offer how-tos, training, or client-only tips.
3. **Acknowledge effort.** People love to be seen for what they're doing right.

Stage 6: Expansion — Growing the Relationship

When you've served well, expansion feels natural—not forced.

Serve, Don't Sell Moves:

1. **Spot new opportunities through listening.** "You mentioned growth—want to explore how we can support that?"
2. **Elevate, don't upsell.** Frame it as helping them reach the *next level*, not spend more.
3. **Co-create the future.** Invite them to shape what comes next.

CHAPTER 12

Retention, Expansion, and Referrals — Turning Service into a Growth Engine

"If you take care of people, people will take care of your business." — Melvin White.

Growth isn't built on speed. It's built on staying power. Anyone can impress a customer once—but keeping them, growing with them, and earning their trust again and again is where real business mastery lives.

Most companies pour their energy into attraction—new ads, new funnels, new faces. But attraction without retention is like filling a leaky bucket. The most innovative leaders know that the real gold is already in their hands: the people who've said yes before and are waiting for another reason to say yes again.

When service becomes your strategy, growth stops feeling like a hustle and starts feeling like a harvest. You begin to see patterns—how one act of follow-up becomes a friendship, how one thoughtful gesture plants the seed for a referral, how one relationship can bloom across decades.

That's how service turns into a growth engine—not through constant chasing, but through consistent caring.

Most companies chase new customers like it's a sprint. But real success comes from the *marathon*—serving the same people so well they never want to leave.
Retention is about consistency. Expansion is about trust. And referrals are the fruit of both.

Retention — Serving Through the Seasons

People don't stay because of what you sell.
They stay because of how you make them *feel* long after the sale.

Call to check in—not to pitch, but to prove you still care.
Follow up on birthdays or business milestones.
Keep small promises sacred—every callback, every text, every honest update matters more than any promotion.

Because service isn't a one-time act; it's a relationship rhythm.

Real-World Example:

My friend Tony Currie and I started at the same cellular stores years ago—back when pagers still buzzed and flip phones were cutting-edge.
While most reps chased commissions, Tony built *connections*.
Today, he's a jeweler with more than twenty years of repeat clients—people who've come back for engagement rings, 10-year anniversaries, 20-year renewals, even 30-year celebrations.

A Business Built on Lifetimes, Not Transactions

Today, more than twenty years later, Tony still serves many of those same customers.
Some bought their first watches from him in the early 2000s. Those same clients returned for engagement rings, then came back again for 10-year anniversaries, 20-year renewals, and 30-year celebrations.

Think about that single relationship spanning three decades, marked by milestones and memories.

He didn't just sell jewelry; he became part of people's stories. Every ring carried a story. Every diamond came with trust.

When I asked Tony how he built that kind of loyalty, he said something I'll never forget:

"You don't sell jewelry; you hold moments. You have to care enough to remember whose story you're holding."

That's the essence of retention, expansion, and referrals—*serving through the seasons.*

Why? Because he never stopped serving. He carried the same mindset from our early sales days: *every interaction is a seed.* And over time, that seed grew into generations of trust.

Tony, owner of Boston's Fine Jewelry

Expansion — Growing with People, Not Off Them

If you serve people well, they'll invite you into the next chapter of their journey.

Expansion happens when you listen for life changes—when clients say, "We're opening a new office," or "My kids are graduating."

Those moments are open doors, not upsells.

Serve, Don't Sell Moves

1. **Spot growth cues.** Listen for transition moments—new seasons create new needs.
2. **Offer alignment, not addition.** "Let's build something that fits where you are now."
3. **Stay a step ahead.** Anticipate, don't chase.

Expansion built on empathy never feels forced—it feels like family.

Referrals — When Service Tells the Story

You'll know you've served well when people start introducing you before you arrive.

Referrals aren't about asking for names; they're about *earning mentions.*

Serve, Don't Sell Moves

1. **Ask after the win, not before it.** "I'm glad this helped. If you know someone facing the same challenge, I'd be honored to serve them too."
2. **Make it easy to refer.** Draft a short intro text or email they can send.
3. **Honor every referral.** Thank them publicly or personally—show gratitude before you show salesmanship.

Stage 7: Referral & Advocacy — When Service Speaks for You

A customer becomes a champion when they feel genuinely cared for. That's when serving turns into marketing.

Serve, Don't Sell Moves:

1. **Ask with gratitude, not guilt.** "If someone you know could benefit like you have, I'd love the chance to serve them too."
2. **Make sharing easy.** Provide a short blurb or sample message they can forward.
3. **Show appreciation publicly.** Recognition reinforces the relationship.

Do: "Thank you for trusting me enough to share my name with someone else."
Don't: "Can you send me three referrals by Friday?"

The Full Circle of Service

When you serve through every stage—from *unaware* to *advocate*—you don't chase loyalty; you cultivate legacy.
People may forget what you sold them, but they'll never forget how you made them feel while they were deciding.

Biblical Principle

> *"Whatever you do, work at it with all your heart, as working for the Lord, not for human masters." — Colossians 3:23 (NIV)*

Serving through the buyer journey is more than good business—it's good stewardship. When you work with heart, humility, and honor, every conversation becomes ministry. And when people feel seen, valued, and helped, your business becomes more than a source of income—it becomes a source of impact.

CHAPTER 13

Storytelling That Serves and Sells

"The most powerful person in the world is the storyteller. The storyteller sets the vision, values, and agenda of an entire generation."
— *Steve Jobs.*

Every product has features. Every business has goals. But what people really buy into is a *story*. Stories are how humans make sense of the world—they're the thread between logic and emotion, between information and inspiration.

A spreadsheet can explain what you do. A story reveals *who you are*. And that difference is everything.

The brands and leaders who rise above the noise aren't the ones shouting the loudest. They're the ones who whisper truth through narrative—who turn their mission into something people can feel. Because when you tell the right story, your audience doesn't just see your product; they see themselves in it.

This chapter is about more than marketing. It's about meaning. It's about learning to tell stories that serve first and sell second— stories that build bridges rather than barriers, trust rather than tension. Because storytelling isn't just a strategy; it's how leaders make people believe again.

Facts inform.
Stories *transform*.
They make strangers lean in, skeptics soften, and buyers believe. The right story doesn't just describe what you sell—it defines why you serve.

When you master storytelling, you stop sounding like a salesperson and start sounding like a servant leader on a mission.

Why Story Matters

People don't connect to data; they connect to *dignity*.
They remember how your story made them feel—hopeful, seen, safe, and inspired.
Numbers fade.
Narratives echo.

Every great brand, movement, or ministry is built on one thing: a story that invites others to believe again.

The Five-Part Story Framework: Problem → Pivot → Promise → Proof → Path

① Problem — Start with the pain

Describe the frustration, fear, or confusion your audience feels right now. Don't polish it. Let it be raw. When they whisper, "That's me," you've earned permission to speak.

② Pivot — Show the turning point

Something—or Someone—decided to change the unavoidable. This is the moment hope entered the room.

③ Promise — Cast the vision

Paint what life could look like *after* the change. People buy progress more than products.

④ Proof — Deliver the evidence

Reveal tangible results through people, not PowerPoints. Let others validate what you claim.

⑤ Path — Show the next step

Invite them forward. End with clarity, not hype: "Here's how you can experience this too."

Keep every story short, sincere, and specific. You're not selling the miracle—you're reminding them miracles still happen.

The Win | When Serving Spoke Louder Than Selling

A small business owner once told me, "We're just price-shopping." I smiled and replied with a story about another company that saved hours each week after switching—how that owner finally made it to his kid's baseball games again. No script. No stats. Just a dad reclaiming his evenings.

Two days later, the "price-shopper" called back:

"That story? That's my life."

Service won where persuasion couldn't.

The Save | When Listening Rebuilt Trust

A client threatened to cancel after a delay. Instead of defending, I said, "Walk me through what happened on your side." He vented. I listened. Then I said, "You deserved better. Let's make it right."

We overnighted replacements and checked in personally. He stayed three more years. People rarely remember excuses—but they always remember empathy.

The Fail | When Exhaustion Eclipsed Empathy

There was a season I was serving everyone but sustaining no one. I kept saying yes—to protect my reputation, not my rest. Eventually, a longtime client said, "You sound tired, Melvin." She was right.

That day I learned: **you can't pour out what you haven't poured in.** Ministry without margin becomes misery. Service loses its spirit when the servant is running on fumes.

Video > Voice | Let People See Themselves in the Story

A written testimonial tells. A video testimonial *shows*.

Encourage clients to record 30-second clips using the Five P's. Ask these simple prompts:

- "What were you struggling with before we met?"
- "What made you decide to act?"
- "What changed afterward?"

Don't chase polish—Chase *truth*.
Real lighting, real language, authentic emotion—those connect faster than any filter.

CHAPTER 14

Is Serving This Way Heavy?

Serving from the heart sounds noble until you realize how much of yourself it costs. You give your time, your creativity, your energy, your peace. You absorb people's stories—their deadlines, fears, disappointments, and sometimes their despair. And if you're not careful, your compassion turns into fatigue, your empathy turns into emptiness, and the very thing that once made you powerful—your heart—starts to feel like a burden.

Biblical Principle

> *"Come to Me, all you who are weary and burdened, and I will give you rest."* — *Matthew 11:28 (NIV)*

But it doesn't have to stay that way.

Selling through serving isn't about becoming a martyr for your mission. It's about creating systems that allow you to love people *and* last in the process. Service is sacred, yes—but it's also strategic. If you burn out, you break the very cycle of care that your business depends on.

Let's unpack how to serve deeply without drowning—how to blend innovative business ideas with ancient biblical truths to sustain both your spirit and your success.

Rest Is a Responsibility, Not Just a Reward

In business, we're taught to grind, to push, to hustle until the sale closes and the numbers line up. But constant motion doesn't equal meaningful progress. Even Jesus, the ultimate servant leader, withdrew from the crowds. He healed, He taught, He gave—but He also disappeared into quiet places to pray, to breathe, to refill.

If the Son of God needed solitude, so do you.

Rest isn't optional; it's operational. It's what keeps you sharp enough to hear the whispers of inspiration—the divine downloads that become the next product, pitch, or partnership. Without rest, creativity dries up. You can't innovate from exhaustion.

Schedule rest like revenue—block it in your calendar and guard it like your best client meeting. Build "margin time" into your business rhythm. That's when your mind resets and your spirit recharges. When you rest well, you don't just recover—you receive new revelation.

Here's a practical truth: your business won't collapse because you took a Sabbath. But your purpose might, if you never pause to reconnect with it.

Boundaries Bless Everybody

Boundaries aren't barriers; they're blueprints for balance. When you serve without structure, you end up resenting the very people you wanted to help. Boundaries don't block love—they preserve it.

You can't serve everyone, and you're not meant to. Jesus didn't heal every person on Earth. He served within divine timing, within human limits, and within clear purpose. That's the model.

Decide when your workday ends and when your phone goes to sleep. Let family have first access to your attention, not leftovers from your day. Use technology with intention—automate what drains you, delegate what distracts you.

One innovative approach is what I call **"service automation with soul."** Automate your follow-ups, thank-you notes, or onboarding messages—but personalize them with warmth and sincerity. Technology should multiply your compassion, not replace it. A simple message that says, *"I was just thinking of you and praying your week's off to a good start,"* can make your client feel seen in a world full of cold emails.

That's not marketing. That's ministry in motion.

Boundaries allow you to serve *better*, not less. They create space for excellence instead of exhaustion. When you're clear about your limits, you give people your best instead of what's left.

Recovery Requires Reflection

In the rush of building and serving, it's easy to forget why you started. You begin to measure worth by outcomes—sales, metrics, milestones—when your true success lives in the lives you've touched.

Keep a **win journal**. Write down the moments that mattered— the client who cried because your product restored her confidence, the family who said your service changed their life, the student who found direction through your words.

Those aren't transactions; they're transformations. And they're proof that service works.

On the weary days, pull out those stories. Let them remind you that your effort isn't wasted. Reflection is recovery. It re-centers your "why" when you feel lost in the "how."

Innovation doesn't only come from brainstorming new strategies—it comes from remembering what already worked when you led with love. Reflection keeps your roots watered. And when your roots are nourished, your results will always follow.

The Truth About Burnout

Here's what no business book tells you: burnout isn't a time-management issue. It's a trust issue.

You've stopped trusting that God can handle things while you rest. You've stopped trusting that the seed will grow even when you're not watching it.

Burnout doesn't happen because you're serving too much. It happens because you've stopped letting yourself *be* served—by God, by rest, by stillness. You keep pouring, pouring, pouring, until your heart runs dry.

Your heart isn't a vending machine for kindness; it's a vessel for purpose. You have to fill before you release, or you must refill after you release. Ideally, you should do both. Always be in a posture of healing, refreshing, and replenishing from the good work of service.

CONCLUSION

The Call to Serve

Let's take a moment to pause and reflect.

We've walked through real stories, timeless principles, hard-earned lessons, and Biblical truths. We've talked about leadership, loyalty, value, and impact. And through it all, one message has remained clear:

> *Success in sales—and in life—is not about how well you sell. It's about how well you serve.*

Let's recap the key truths:

- **Principles before tactics.** When you operate from a foundation of service, everything else aligns.

- **Serve first, and sales will follow.** People buy from those they know, like, and trust—and trust is built through consistent, genuine service.

- **Leadership is about lifting others.** Whether you're managing a team, leading a business, or influencing a community, great leaders are great servants.

- **Know your people individually.** We're not all wired the same. True leaders learn who's in the room, then lead accordingly.

- **The reward is in the relationship.** Trips, awards, and recognition are nice—but the real win is knowing you made a difference in someone's life.

This isn't about being soft. It's about being **strong enough to care**, bold enough to listen, and humble enough to put others first.

Whether you're in sales, in leadership, in ministry, or in your own family—serving is your superpower.

As Jesus said,

> *"The greatest among you will be your servant." (Matthew 23:11)*

You don't need a title to serve. You don't need a stage, a spotlight, or a script.

Final Call to Action: Let the Shift Begin

If you've made it this far, I want to thank you. Not just for reading, but for being open to something different. Something **real**. Something **life-changing**.

Now, it's your turn.

- Start listening more intentionally.
- Start asking how you can solve before you sell.
- Start leading with compassion, not just with pressure.
- Start looking for ways to add value in every conversation.
- Start focusing less on being impressive and more on being impactful.

Start serving.

Because when you stop chasing the sale…
When you stop making it about you…
When you start serving with purpose, passion, and heart…
That's when everything changes.

> *"Success is not measured by how many*
> *people you lead—it's measured by how well*
> *you serve the people you lead."*
> *— (Your name here… because this is your*
> *story now.)*

Thank you for joining me on this journey.
Now go—**stop selling, start serving—and watch what happens next.**

A Personal Note from the Author

When I first set out to write this book, I thought it would be a story about my life. Something close to an autobiography. And trust me—that book is coming.

But as I sat down to reflect, to write, and to pray, something shifted in me. I realized that while my life has been full of experiences, blessings, trials, and lessons, what mattered most right now was the message—not just the memories.

Because life is short, purpose is precious. And time is limited.

And if you're going to spend time reading something I've written, I want it to leave you with more than a few facts about me. I want to add value to you. I want it to make you think, make you reflect, and maybe even inspire you to lead and live differently.

Most of my adult life has been spent in sales—from commission-only jobs to corporate leadership roles, from knocking on doors to sitting in boardrooms. Along the way, I've made great friends, and, if I'm being honest, probably a few enemies too.

(If that's you—please forgive me.)

But more than the deals, more than the quotas, more than the titles—what I'm most grateful for are the people I've helped.

And it wasn't always about what I was selling.
Sometimes, the real impact came simply from being who I am—showing up with integrity. Listening. Encouraging, telling the truth, and/or just being there.

If this book has reminded you that you have the power to serve, to lead, and to leave people better than you found them—then it's done its job.

You don't need a title to lead.
You don't need a product to serve.
You need to start—**right where you are, with what you have.**

So… stop selling.
Start serving.
And watch what God does next.

Reflection Questions

Thank you for allowing me to share this part of my journey with you.

Now it's your turn. Take a moment to sit with these. Journal your answers. Talk them out with someone you trust. Let them guide your next step forward.

1. Am I more focused on closing deals or creating value?

2. How do I show up for the people I lead or serve?

3. Have I been listening more than I've been speaking?

4. What does servant leadership look like in my current role or business?

5. When was the last time I helped someone without expecting anything in return?

6. Who has served me well in my journey—and how can I honor or learn from them?

7. If someone were to describe my leadership style, would they say I serve or control?

8. What's one habit I can change today to lead with more purpose and less pressure?

Recommended Resources

To continue growing as a servant leader and value-driven professional, here are some books, talks, and voices that have deeply impacted my journey. I hope they speak to you, too.

📚 Books

- *Jesus, CEO* by Laurie Beth Jones

- *The 7 Habits of Highly Effective People* by Stephen R. Covey

- *Uncommon* by Tony Dungy

- *Live Your Dreams* by Les Brown

- *From the Trash Man to the Cash Man* by Myron Golden

- *Resilience* by Eric Thomas

- *Abundance Now* by Lisa Nichols

- *Leading an Inspired Life* by Jim Rohn

- *The Bible* – Start with Proverbs and the Gospels (especially the words of Jesus)

Speakers & Mentors to Follow

- Les Brown

- Myron Golden

- Lisa Nichols

- Eric Thomas (ET the Hip Hop Preacher)

- Jim Rohn (archived talks)

- Tony Dungy

- Stephen Covey

- Zig Ziglar

- John Maxwell

AI Tools That Can Help You Serve Smarter

"Tools don't make trust. People do. But the right tools can give you more time to build it."

Below are a few cutting-edge tools that bring these principles to life:

1. NotebookLM — Your Personal Knowledge Partner
⚲ https://notebooklm.google

Developed by Google, NotebookLM is an AI research and note-organizing platform that helps you upload documents, transcripts, or meeting notes and then ask natural-language questions about them. It creates summaries, insights, and connections from your own content—perfect for prepping before client calls or writing internal reports.

2. Gemini (Google AI) — The All-in-One Intelligent Assistant

⚲ https://gemini.google.com

Gemini integrates deeply with Google Workspace—Docs, Gmail, and Sheets—to automate routine tasks like drafting proposals, analyzing spreadsheets, and suggesting next steps. Its contextual understanding makes it ideal for leaders managing multiple accounts or projects simultaneously.

3. ChatGPT by OpenAI — Your Conversational Co-Creator

⚲ https://chat.openai.com

ChatGPT has evolved far beyond simple text generation. It can now summarize meetings, brainstorm campaigns, generate code or copy, and even analyze uploaded files. Future versions are expected to integrate directly with business dashboards, CRM systems, and voice interactions—turning insights into real-time action.

4. Apollo.io — AI-Powered Prospecting & Outreach

⚲ https://www.apollo.io

Apollo.io combines a massive, verified contact database with AI-driven engagement tools. It helps sales professionals identify qualified leads, craft personalized outreach sequences, and automate follow-ups—all while tracking engagement analytics in real time. It's one of the most potent examples of AI directly impacting the sales process.

Together, these tools form an *AI ecosystem for service*—giving you the research power of a team, the speed of automation, and the insight of a strategist.

Use them wisely.
Let them handle the busy work so you can focus on the heart work.